P9-DNC-100

HAND COLORING BLACK & WHITE PHOTOGRAPHY

An introduction and step-by-step guide

GLOUCESTER MASSACHUSETTS

ROCKPORT PUBLISHERS

Laurie Klein

All Step-by-Step Photography by Laurie Klein

CONTENTS

△ Hand color to give a photograph a "painterly quality."

INTRODUCTION

Can you paint or draw? I can't! I'm intimidated by a paintbrush, and sketching has never been my strong suit. And yet I am regarded as a leader in hand coloring photographs. How do I do it? Well, in addition to having a good eye for composition and a technique that works wonders for me (as it will for you), I think of each photograph I'm going to hand color as a page out of a coloring book—and I color within the lines!

I have been a fine-art photographer for twenty-five years and a photographic educator for over eighteen years. I have taught hand coloring to photographers, artists, and craftspeople and to children as young as kindergarten age. Many of my students who had prior experience in hand coloring said they found the process to be relatively complicated. The method I use, however, is very easy and produces beautiful results. And the materials needed are readily available—you probably have most of them already.

Hand coloring photographs was popular in the 1800s, and recently I have observed a resurgence in this art form. Perhaps it is due to the popularity of memory books. Our photographs of family and friends represent our personal history. Hand coloring these photographs results in a unique and timeless piece of artwork. In my commercial wedding and portrait photography business, many of my clients come to me because my images are a marriage of photography and a "painterly quality" created by hand coloring. Indeed, hand-colored photos are a lasting and creative expression of favorite memories.

Hand coloring is also a great project to do with children. Children are extremely creative, whether they're hand coloring photographs they have taken themselves or that someone else has taken. Let the creative child within you surface, and feel free to experiment. You can't make a mistake, so have some fun.

△ Use colored pencils to enhance the nuances of a complicated image.

WATERFORD TOWNSHIP
PUBLIC LIBRARY

092122

THE BASICS

Sanford's Prismacolor pencils were used in many of the demonstrations in this book. Prismacolor pencils are made in a variety of colors and have a soft lead that will not scratch the surface (emulsion) of the print. Most colored pencils, however, will work just fine for hand coloring.

Colored pencils are great for hand coloring photographs because they're not intimidating like a paintbrush can be—you don't need special skills to use them. We've all been using pencils for most of our lives, and you probably even have some colored pencils around the house. A wonderful part of working with colored pencils is that

mistakes can be removed with a cotton swab moistened with a very small amount of water, making this a very forgiving medium for hand coloring.

In some of the demonstrations, a solution of turpentine and vegetable oil is used as a solvent for the colored pencils. The solvent is used to create a wash of color so the pencil strokes are not apparent on the print. Applied with a cotton swab, the oil allows the color to move around, creating the wash, and the turpentine cuts the oil slick on the print. This technique produces a transparent color that doesn't obscure the photograph; the color appears to be a part of the image rather than sitting on the surface of the print. Turpentine-and-oil solution can also be used to remove excess color. But be careful not to use too much solution. A very little goes a long way, as is explained in this book.

When learning to hand color, be sure to make multiple prints of the image being hand colored. This way you can experiment and compare the effects of different procedures and mediums. Keep records of each step so you can duplicate results you like.

LEMON YELLOW

FLESH

MAGENTA

CYAN

GREEN

ORANGE

△ Colored pencils are ideal for hand coloring because they don't require special skills to use them. And even just a handful of colors, such as the ones shown here, can produce vivid results.

Materials

Other than the photographic prints, you probably already have many of the materials required for hand coloring. Colored pencils are essential. Either use what you already have, or buy a small basic set of pencils. The basic set will include the colors needed to get started and can be mixed to create other colors. Besides, specific colors can always be bought individually at a later date. You may also want to buy Sanford's Blender Pencil. It's useful for keeping two side-by-side colors from overlapping to create a third color. It's also helpful in cleaning up areas of unwanted color, and it can be used to make the transition from one color to another smooth.

Other necessary supplies include: a tray; cotton swabs; cotton balls; toothpicks; transparent tape; a pencil sharpener; tongs; a small container for water; matte spray; vegetable oil; odorless turpentine (or a turpentine substitute); and a small glass bottle, preferably with a narrow neck and a top (don't use rubber lids—the turpentine in the turpentine-and-oil solution will dissolve the rubber). Optional are a small glass or heavy plastic measuring cup, sepia toner, and nylon or soft, lint-free gloves.

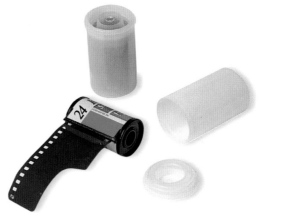

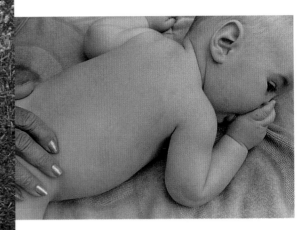

△ 400-speed film

△ High-speed infrared film

Film Types

The majority of photographs that are hand colored are taken with black-and-white film and are printed on black-and-white photographic paper. (A black-and-white print can be made from a color negative, but the results will be different.)

The photographs in this book were taken with three different film speeds: 100, 400, and high-speed infrared film. Which black-and-white film to use depends on the subject matter as well as the lighting conditions, the time of year, and whether you are shooting indoors or outdoors. When photographing outside in bright sunlight or even on bright overcast days in warmer weather, use a slower film speed, like 100 or 125. These films have less grain and, in photographs of people, will render soft, smooth skin tones. For overcast, cloudier days, during the winter months, or when inside, use a faster film like 400, which is a bit grainy. In very low light situations without a flash, experiment with high-speed films, such as 1000 and above. Read the data sheet that comes with the film to become familiar with its characteristics.

Different kinds of film yield different effects or can evoke certain moods. For a romantic feel, try using a high-speed infrared film, which will produce a grainy look. Infrared film is a technical film that lends itself beautifully to hand coloring because it produces so many light/highlight tones.

◁ Photographs with a matte surface
are ideal for hand coloring.

Print Surfaces

Photographic papers come in a variety of sizes, surfaces, types, and tones. Paper surface should be selected based on the materials being used to hand color. Matte surfaces, for instance, work the best regardless of the medium, but many materials won't adhere to a high-gloss surface. In fact, if you'll be using pencils, a flat matte surface is required. Oils can be used on a flat or semi-matte/pearl surface, and acrylics can be used on any surface. To make a print with a glossy or semi-matte/pearl surface suitable for hand coloring, spray it with matte spray to give it "tooth," or texture.

Print sizes vary. The easiest to hand color, and the size I recommend for beginners, is an 8" x 10" (20 cm x 25 cm) print. Anything smaller than this size will require more detailed work. Plus, larger prints are more expensive and take longer to color. After mastering hand coloring an 8" x 10" (20 cm x 25 cm) print, try working on a larger print. The results can be spectacular.

Photographic papers are either fiber-based or resin-coated (R/C). Photos printed on fiber-based paper are somewhat easier to hand color, and colored pencils appear slightly brighter on them. However, this paper is more expensive, and it takes longer to make a print on it than on resin-coated paper, which should be taken into account if you're doing the printing yourself. Keep track of the kind of paper you're using. Tonal qualities vary by manufacturer. Some papers are warmer or cooler toned, and some have a slight color cast. These characteristics will affect the results of hand coloring.

Shooting Images to Hand Color

Any subject matter and type of photograph can be hand colored. Landscapes, people, animals, architecture, interiors, vacation photos, or even scenes staged with props and costumes work well. The more you enjoy the subject matter and the photograph, the more fun you will have hand coloring the print.

Keep in mind, though, that the sharper the image, the better defined the potential hand-coloring areas will be. Areas that hand color the best are the light and highlight areas; color applied to dark areas of a print won't show up very well. Since the light/highlight areas are the most obvious areas to hand color, some hand colorists print their photos slightly lighter than usual.

Photographing with black-and-white film is different from using color film. All colors become a shade of gray, black, or white. If you're posing a shot, use props that are light in color, and have the subjects wear light-colored clothing. Since you are the artist, if you want the color of someone's sweater to be red, then have that person wear a pastel or very light-colored sweater and then color it the desired red after printing the photo. Learning how black-and-white film sees reality takes practice. Sometimes squinting or wearing dark sunglasses that are neutral in color helps simulate how the film reads colors.

Using Images of Your Own

Test existing black-and-white photographs you'd like to hand color to see if the surface of the prints will "take" the colored pencils. Take a bright-colored pencil and make two marks: one in the white border that surrounds the image and the other on a blank piece of paper. Compare the two marks to see if they look similar. If they do, then the print can be hand colored. If the pencil barely makes a mark on the print or comes off when rubbed, then the print surface is not suitable. (Remember, the mark can be erased with a small amount of water and a cotton swab.) In the latter case, use matte spray to give the print tooth (see "Print Surfaces"). One note on matte spray: If you overwork a sprayed print or use too much solution on it, the spray can come off in areas, and in those areas the color will not adhere.

When working with snapshots or vintage photographs, you may not want to use the original print. Instead, go to a lab and have either a copy negative or computer-generated negative made. Then have a black-and-white print made from that on matte-surface paper. You may have to go to a professional lab for this because most color labs print black-and-white film on color paper, and the tones and the surfaces will not be good for hand coloring.

Color prints are also an option. Color negatives can be printed on black-and-white paper, but the prints will need to be sprayed first if they are not printed on matte-surface paper.

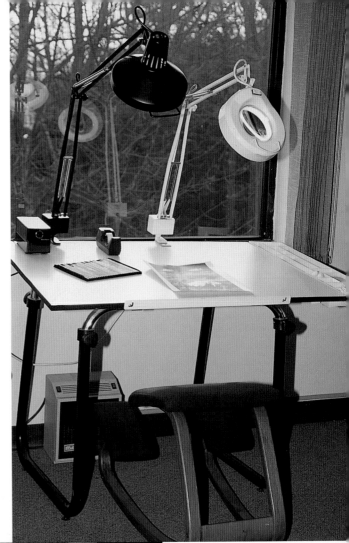

▷ Look for a smooth work surface, such as a drafting table or a regular table covered with a piece of acrylic or smooth mat board.

Work Area

Start with a smooth work surface. If it isn't smooth, the print will pick up its texture when it is hand colored, just as if it were a rubbing of the table. If you like to work at an angle, try a drafting table or a portable drafting table that can be placed on an existing tabletop. Drafting tables, which are adjustable, are available at most office-supply stores. To work on a flat surface, use a piece of acrylic or smooth mat board on a regular table.

Some of the materials used to hand color are toxic, so if you're working in your kitchen, be sure to keep your work area separate from food-preparation areas. Ventilation is also something to keep in mind. When using turpentine (in the turpentine-and-oil solution), it's a good idea to use an air purifier or keep a window open. When working outside,

avoid bright sunlight because the heat from the sun could curl the prints and make your pencil tips more apt to break.

Good lighting is essential in a work area. Natural light works well, as do lights that have both a fluorescent tube and a tungsten bulb. These lights give a natural, balanced light and are very bright. If working outside, choose a shady area.

◁ *Joanne, Kelly, Barton, and Stephanie*
by Laurie Klein
This photograph was over-matted with a
French mat. Some of the colors used in the
photo were also applied to the French mat.

the photo was printed on matte or semi-matte paper. Also, the small amount of residual oil from the solution or the waxy residue that colored pencils sometimes leave will not be visible.

Double mat your print, or at least place a mat over it to avoid contact with the glass. If the glass from the frame is flush against the print, the hand coloring will be transferred from the print to the glass. Using an over mat or double mat makes the piece look very professional.

I don't recommend dry mounting the print with a hot or cold press because the heat and rubbing necessary in this process can affect the hand coloring. Don't use an album that has acetate overlays. They can destroy photographic prints over a period of time. Your work of art is one of a kind and therefore irreplaceable. To make copies, either have a color laser copy made or have a lab make a color copy negative, from which a color print can be made.

Presentation

I do not recommend spraying a print after it has been toned and hand colored. The more chemicals (other than toners) that are applied to a print, the greater the chance it will deteriorate. Instead, try framing the photograph. This will protect it from moisture and dust, both of which could ruin the hand coloring that you have spent so much time creating.

Many people don't like the look of matte print paper because it has a dull, flat appearance. But once the print is behind glass, you won't be able to tell whether

▷ *Untitled*
by Laurie Klein
This photo is over-matted. The color of
the frame echoes that of the barn.

◁ This photo is framed very simply with
a beveled over-mat.

BASIC HOW-TO DEMONSTRATION

MIXING COLORS

A color wheel, which can be made or purchased, is helpful in understanding how to mix colors, such as making green out of blue and yellow. Harmonious colors are located next to one another on the color wheel. For example, red and orange are harmonious colors. Conversely, colors opposite each other on the wheel, such as red and green, are called complementary colors. They create a bold, dramatic feel, which is a much different mood. When complementary colors are mixed together, however, a muddy color results.

Colored pencils can be mixed directly on the print or in the white border area of the print. Using the blender pencil, blend the colors where they overlap, producing a third color. Another option is to use a separate piece of plain white photographic paper as a palette. Mix colors with the turpentine-and-oil solution and then transfer them to the print using a cotton swab.

CHOOSING COLORS

Choosing colors can be the hardest and yet most enjoyable part of the hand-coloring process. There are so many approaches. A photo can be colored realistically, interpreted with colors, or made to look surrealistic by using colors that are far from realistic and that allow the imagination to soar. Adding color to a black-and-white photograph establishes a mood or feeling. Always look at the image and get a sense of what you'd like to communicate. Hand coloring takes an image one step further, and the colors directly affect the message. If the goal is to make the print bold and graphic, for example, use vibrant colors.

It's important to maintain your colored pencils. Sharpen the end of the pencil that doesn't bear the name or number of the color so you'll know which one it is when you need to replace it. Also, make sure the tips aren't too sharp or long. To color large areas, use Prismacolor Art Stix.

Red, orange, and yellow are warm colors.

red + blue = purple

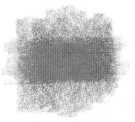

red + yellow = orange

Greens and blues are cool colors.

yellow + blue = green

Red and green are complementary colors.

Hand Coloring a Photo

Now it's time to jump in, take a pencil in hand, and actually color the photograph. But keep it simple. Sometimes the least amount of color creates the most interesting result. Remember that hand coloring an area changes the composition, so after choosing the first area to hand color, check the compositional balance. This may influence which area you choose to color next and how you color it.

Experiment with a solution that is equal parts vegetable oil and odorless turpentine. It's important to prepare this solution properly. If the print is too oily looking, there's too much oil in the solution; if all the color comes off, then there's too much turpentine (turpentine removes color). Store the solution in a small bottle with a lid. It will last for a long time. Don't leave the solution uncovered, though, because the

turpentine will evaporate and the mixture will then be out of balance. Use as little solution as possible, and try not to use it too often. In small areas, for example, rubbing the color with a cotton swab is sufficient to smooth out the pencil strokes and remove waxy buildup.

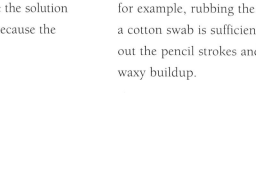

△ This photo was chosen because there is no single focal point; each blade of grass has equal importance. Choose one blade of grass and color it in using the spring green pencil. (It will not be necessary to use solution.) Now the emphasis is on that one blade of grass.

△ Here, the whole image was colored with the same green pencil. Don't color each blade of grass individually; it will take
too long. Instead, create a color wash by using a small
amount of solution and a cotton ball. Solution was applied to
the left side of the photo, whereas the color on the right side
of the photo was not blended and the pencil marks are still
apparent. Leaving the marks unblended makes the color
appear to sit on top of the print instead of be a part of it.

No solution

▽ In this photograph, lighter, brighter colors were added to the grass in the foreground to give the image a three-dimensional look. Other greens were used, and pinks and oranges were blended with the spring green to create a warmer green. These variations of green make the image more interesting.

△ Color to capture the mood.

PEOPLE

Most of the photographs you already have are probably snapshots of family members and friends. You may have a lifetime of memories filed away—family vacations, weddings, birthdays, and anniversaries, or perhaps friends just having fun. Maybe you even have vintage photographs of ancestors. Have you ever wondered what else could be done with these photographs? Hand-colored photographs make wonderful, personal gifts. Hand coloring a photo gives the image a timeless quality and combines the realism of photography with the artistry of painting. With the popularity of memory albums and scrapbooks, many people are coloring vintage black-and-white and contemporary family photographs to preserve their family history. Chances are, most of your photographs are color prints or vintage black-and-white prints. Before you start to color, have "copy negatives" made, so that you can have multiple prints of the same photo and can preserve the original. Use the copies to experiment—try several different applications of color to achieve different results.

▷ Color for realism.

▷ Color photos to remember the moment.

Working with Photographs of People

When selecting a photograph to color, seek images with a lot of highlight areas (places that show white or a pale tone on the photograph). Images with lots of highlights work best for hand coloring. Selecting an image that is a close-up of someone's face allows you to color in skin tones or apply color like makeup. If the color is applied subtly, you can mimic the appearance of an "old-fashioned portrait." Color applied more boldly creates a contemporary effect.

Photographs of people in landscapes ("environmental" portraits) give you the opportunity to color both people and nature. Where you apply the color is a matter of artistic choice. Start with the part of the image that you feel is most important. It will be easiest to leave small details for last, after applying the main colors.

▷ Outdoor photos allow
you to color both
people and landscapes.

Color is powerful. Even a little color
added to a photo will change it entirely.
Different colors create different moods:
Reds, yellows, and oranges will make an
image warm and inviting, while blues
and greens produce a colder, fresher
look. Use more than one shade of a
color for a more natural effect. Blending
and layering warm or cool colors will
add dimension and realism.

▷ Emphasize the
foreground by
adding color.

If you want an area to stand out, try
using a color that is opposite to the sur-
rounding color—red against a green
background, for example. Conversely,
applying heavy layers of color will flatten the area somewhat, and put more
emphasis on color than on the content
of the image, making it less like a photograph and more like modern art.

▷ Look for images
with a lot of
white areas.

△ The graphic qualities
and bold shapes of this
photograph make it very
appealing to hand color.

Hand Coloring a Contemporary Photo

GETTING STARTED

Try hand coloring photographs of people that are unique or abstract, as this image is. For example, a people photo without actual faces in it can be interesting and full of feeling. People often assume that when photographing someone, they should place the subject's head in the center of the viewfinder. But feel free to try something different. Play with the whole frame; move in close and place the subject in the corner of the frame. (See "The Basics" for more on shooting images to hand color.)

MATERIALS

- black-and-white print on matte-surface paper
- colored pencils: flesh, blush, scarlet lake, true blue, olive green, metallic copper, imperial violet, green bice, orange, apple green, lemon yellow, violet blue
- cotton balls
- cotton swabs
- turpentine-and-oil solution
- Art Stix

FLESH   IMPERIAL VIOLET

BLUSH   GREEN BICE

SCARLET LAKE   ORANGE

TRUE BLUE   APPLE GREEN

OLIVE GREEN   LEMON YELLOW

METALLIC COPPER   VIOLET BLUE

△ 1

Using the flesh pencil, color both babies' legs. Rub with a cotton swab to smooth in color (solution won't be necessary). Using the blush pencil, color the soles of the babies' feet, once again using the cotton swab to smooth the color in. Now use the flesh pencil again, moving from the legs to the soles of the feet, so it is not apparent where one color ends and the other begins. This is called "feathering."

▷ 2

Color the outfit on the baby in the upper-right section with the scarlet lake pencil. Use a cotton swab and a small amount of solution to smooth in the color so that no pencil marks are visible. Using the true-blue pencil, color the outfit on the baby in the lower-left section. Smooth the color in with a cotton swab and a small amount of solution, just as with the previous baby. Use a dry cotton swab on both outfits to remove any residual color or solution. To make the outfits deeper in color, apply a second coat. Use a dry cotton swab to smooth in the color.

TIP

○ Try using an olive-green Prismacolor Art Stix for the grass. Art Stix are terrific for coloring large areas.

◁ 3

Using the olive-green pencil, color the grass area. In the areas around the babies' bodies and clothing, use a small amount of solution on a cotton swab to smooth in the color. For the larger areas, use a cotton ball with a small amount of solution to smooth in the color. Color the blades of grass in front of the babies' feet with a sharpened olive-green pencil.

▷ 4

Use the orange, imperial violet, metallic copper, and green bice pencils on the grass to give it more depth. Select a few different blades of grass and color them individually for a more natural look. Smooth the color in with a cotton swab.

VARIATION

Complementary colors are perfect for making a statement.

1. Don't add any color to the babies' feet. Use the scarlet lake pencil for the grass to create a surrealistic effect. Use turpentine-and-oil solution on a cotton swab to smooth in the color.

2. With the apple-green pencil, color a few select blades of grass. Blend with a cotton swab. The red (scarlet lake) and green, which are complementary colors, add up to a bold statement.

3. Color the outfit on the baby in the upper-right section using the lemon-yellow pencil. Apply a small amount of solution to a cotton swab and smooth in the color. Using the violet blue pencil, color the outfit of the baby in the lower-left section. Use a small amount of solution on a swab for blending.

△ This image has a great deal of
mood, especially since the bride
and flower girl are looking at
one another and not directly into
the camera.

◁ The way the gray stonework and
stairs contrast with the pale
tones of the garments and flowers
makes this a wonderful image to
hand color.

Creating a Romantic Atmosphere

GETTING STARTED

This photograph was chosen because it is a candid depiction of the bride, ring bearer, and flower girl. They are the main subjects in the photograph, but the flowers and greenery can have as much emphasis if hand colored. Hand coloring them also strengthens the balance of the composition, echoing the triangular shape made by the bride and the children.

MATERIALS

- black-and-white print on matte-surface paper
- colored pencils: deco pink, olive green, lavender, sand, pink, salmon pink, brite purple, orange, lemon yellow, grayed lavender, true green, light peach/flesh, blush, true blue, raw umber, clay rose, terra-cotta, nonphoto blue
- cotton balls
- toothpicks
- cotton swabs
- turpentine-and-oil solution
- blender pencil
- sepia toner

DECO PINK / GRAYED LAVENDER

OLIVE GREEN / TRUE GREEN

LAVENDER / LIGHT PEACH/FLESH

SAND / BLUSH

PINK / TRUE BLUE

SALMON PINK / RAW UMBER

BRITE PURPLE / CLAY ROSE

ORANGE / TERRA-COTTA

LEMON YELLOW / NONPHOTO BLUE

△ 1

Sepia-tone the print. (See "Advanced Techniques.") Use the deco pink pencil to color the top and bottom of the bride's dress, applying very small amounts of solution to smooth in the color. Use the same pencil for the flower girl's hairpiece. Smooth the color in with a fresh cotton swab.

△ **2**

Color the foliage with the olive-green pencil. Use a small amount of solution to smooth in the color.

TIPS

○ To remove a color, use a tooth-pick with a very small amount of water on it. Wait a few minutes for the water to dry (the color won't adhere if the print is wet), and then reapply color.

○ To soften the line where two colors meet, try using the blender pencil.

▷ **3**

Using the lavender pencil, color the satin wrap on the stems of the bouquet. Use the sand pencil to color the large flower. Also use the sand pencil on select smaller flowers to balance the large flower. Use the pink, salmon pink, and brite purple pencils to color the remaining flowers. A little solution may be necessary for blending. Use a toothpick wrapped tightly in cotton with some solution for blending small areas, or try using the blender pencil instead. Use the olive-green pencil to color the darker areas around and within the flowers to add depth.

◁ 4

Hand coloring is a way to strengthen or even alter the composition of a photo. Use the sand, lemon yellow, salmon pink, pink, and grayed lavender for the flowers on the steps. Try layering colors, such as yellow over pink. Use the true green for some of the foliage in the bouquets and olive green to add depth between and within the flowers. These colors, which are from a slightly different palette than those used in the bride's bouquet, draw the viewer's attention up and around the steps.

VARIATION

Bold hues can heighten the sense of romance.

1. Use the light peach/flesh pencil to color all skin areas. Then, using a very small amount of solution on a toothpick wrapped in a cotton ball, smooth in the color.

2. Moving the pink pencil in a circular motion, color the cheek areas. Blend with a fresh cotton swab so the color doesn't appear to be on top of the skin tone, but rather looks like it's a part of it. Use a sharpened blush pencil to color in the lips.

3. The true-blue pencil was used on the boy's eyes. The girl's hair was colored with streaks of lemon yellow in the lighter areas and raw umber in the darker strands of hair.

4. Use the lemon yellow to lightly color the lighter strands of the boy's hair to highlight and add luster, creating depth and balancing his hair with the girl's.

5. Color the bride's earrings with the sand pencil. Use the clay-rose pencil and solution to color the background stone and steps.

6. Use the olive-green pencil and solution for all the foliage in the lower left and upper right. The terra-cotta pencil can be used on a few leaves; blend with a dry cotton swab for depth.

7. On the boy's and girl's outfits, use the nonphoto blue. Experiment with different colors in the flowers, using bold complementary colors.

△ Begin with a copy of
your favorite black-
and-white portrait.

▷ Colored pencils make soft,
muted hues, so prints with
lots of light tones work best.
Details in the dress give you
areas in which to be creative
and experiment with color.

Hand Coloring a Vintage Photograph

GETTING STARTED

Start by choosing a black-and-white print with a matte surface. Any image you have on hand can be used. If all your photographs are in color, have a black-and-white copy negative made and then printed on matte-surface paper. Most photo labs can easily make one for you. Likewise, if you have selected a vintage black-and-white photograph, it is a good idea to have a copy negative and print made. Then you can work on the re-print rather than coloring the original. Sepia-toning your prints will give them an antique look and can make even the most recent photographs seem vintage. When choosing a photograph to color, remember that lighter tones will show colors best.

MATERIALS

- black-and-white print on matte-surface paper
- colored pencils: flesh, pink, blush, scarlet lake, true blue, lemon yellow, canary yellow, mineral orange, crimson red, lavender, marine green, white, vermilion red, green bice
- cotton balls
- toothpicks
- cotton swabs
- turpentine-and-oil solution
- sepia toner

FLESH

MINERAL ORANGE

PINK

CRIMSON RED

BLUSH

LAVENDER

SCARLET LAKE

MARINE GREEN

TRUE BLUE

VERMILION RED

LEMON YELLOW

GREEN BICE

CANARY YELLOW

 1

First, sepia-tone the print. (See "Advanced Techniques.") Then, choose the most important areas and color these first. For this sepia-toned print, a flesh-colored pencil was used for the skin. Work with a back-and-forth motion to fill the whole area with color, then gently rub in the color with a cotton swab. For small areas, use part of a cotton ball wrapped around a toothpick.

△ **2**

A sharpened scarlet lake pencil adds
brilliant color to the lips. A sharp-
pointed true-blue pencil accents the
eyes. Create contour in the cheek
area with the pink pencil, or, if you
want a look that is more subtle, you
can use the blush pencil. To add
accents to the hair, try using the
lemon-yellow pencil in the lighter
areas. Wipe away any excess pencil
wax with a cotton swab.

▽ **3**

Using light, even strokes, color the clothing next. Dab a tiny amount of solution
on the print with a cotton swab. With a
different cotton swab, use a circular
motion to rub in the color; aim for a
uniform, transparent wash.

TIPS

○ For more vibrant skin tones,
  mix crimson red and white
  instead of using the flesh pencil.

○ Erase mistakes with cotton
  swabs and small amounts
  of water.

○ Make sure the entire area is
  filled with color before rubbing
  with the swab.

○ Go over areas twice to
  enhance color saturation. Use
  a new swab for each color.

○ If dark areas look shiny, swab
  them with a little water to
  dull them.

Contour the folds in the clothing with an accent color, such as mineral orange, to create depth. To finish, use crimson, lavender, and marine green pencils on details such as the garland of flowers. The same colors are also used on neckline to give the image harmony. True-blue pencil in the background and scarlet lake hues in the rug complete this hand-colored photograph.

VARIATION

A different palette creates
a completely different mood.

1. Color skin tones as in step one.
2. Use vermilion red to color the hair, then accent with canary yellow in the highlight areas for depth.
3. True blue and green bice create heightened contrast in the clothing. Green in the folds of the dress brings the color up into the bodice for continuity.
4. Use vermilion red on accents, such as the flower trim here.
5. Shade crimson on the background and blend smooth with a little solution on a cotton ball. On the areas close to the body, you may need to use a swab for better control. Canary yellow works well for small highlight areas in the background.

△ Hand coloring brings
out the textures.

▷ This image had a great
deal of mood even
before it was hand
colored.

Hand Coloring for Realism

GETTING STARTED

The texture of the tree trunk in this photograph made it an interesting selection to hand color. Different colors were used to create even more texture. Hand coloring everything except the young boy distinguishes him from the background, which also makes the photo look more three-dimensional.

MATERIALS

- black-and-white print on matte-surface paper

- colored pencils: spring green, terra-cotta, sienna brown, pink, canary yellow, poppy red, metallic copper, carmine red, Copenhagen blue, flesh, crimson red, peacock blue, sand, blush

- cotton swabs

- turpentine-and-oil solution

SPRING GREEN   CARMINE RED

TERRA-COTTA   COPENHAGEN BLUE

SIENNA BROWN   FLESH

PINK   CRIMSON RED

CANARY YELLOW   PEACOCK BLUE

POPPY RED   SAND

METALLIC COPPER   BLUSH

▷ **1**

Apply an even wash of spring green on the grass. To create the wash, apply the color and then smooth it in with a cotton swab soaked in a small amount of solution. Take your time when smoothing in the color so that it will be consistent throughout the grass. Continue to use fresh cotton swabs until you get an even wash. To clean areas where the color has bled, use a fresh cotton swab and a small amount of water.

▷ 2

Color the larger tree using the terra-cotta pencil. Using a small amount of solution on a cotton swab, smooth in the color. Use the sienna brown for the trees in the background. Blend with a small amount of solution.

◁ 3

To create more depth, use the pink pencil to color random areas of the grass. The mixture of the coolness of the green in the grass and the warmth of the pink adds depth. Smooth in the color with a cotton swab.

TIP

○ Use the sunlight in a photograph as a guide when choosing an image to hand color. In this photograph, for example, it appears to be late afternoon. The shadows are long and angular and create warm sunlight on the tree trunk for contours and depth.

◁ 4

Use the canary yellow and poppy red pencils to color the lighter (highlighted) areas of the tree. (Tree bark is never just one color. Using other colors makes the trunk appear three-dimensional. Blend with a dry cotton swab.) Color the dirt area in the grass and the other shadow areas with the metallic copper pencil, using a small back-and-forth motion. This adds contrast (by making it darker) and warms up the area. Use a cotton swab to lightly rub the color in.

VARIATION

Experiment with bold colors on dyed or toned prints.

This photograph was dyed using tea. (See "Advanced Techniques.") Stronger colors are necessary for prints that are heavily dyed or toned.

1. Use carmine red, a warm color, for the pants, adding crimson red in the darker folds to show the contours.
2. Color the sweatshirt with Copenhagen blue, a cool color. Use peacock blue in the folds.
3. Use the sand pencil for the highlights in the boy's hair. Flesh can be used on his face and hand, with blush added on his cheek.

PLACES

Photographs of landscapes and nature are wonderful to hand color. Black-and-white photographs of sunsets, for example, can be hand colored to create a romantic or serene feel. Photographs of clouds taken before or after a storm also can be the basis of a dramatic hand-colored image.

Another advantage of landscapes is that they lend themselves to a three-dimensional look. Use darker and more saturated colors in the foreground and lighter and less saturated ones for objects that appear farther away from the viewer. Coloring the sky area blue adds to the effect of distant objects receding. Choose a palette to create the desired mood.

Other possibilities include photographing pets outdoors. Then there are flowers and wild animals, although a macro setting or close-up attachment may be necessary to photograph flowers (many zoom lenses have macro settings as a feature). Try photographing your house and then hand coloring it and sending it as a postcard. Boats and interesting architecture are excellent subjects for hand coloring. Amusement parks, with their bright lights and action, are great to photograph and hand color. Experiment with slow and fast shutter speeds to capture the energy of the rides, then use vibrant colors to color the image. It's also fun to hand color photographs of still lifes arranged using fruit, flowers, and shells.

You may already have these types of photographs at home. Just remember that when picking out prints to hand color—or when actually photographing images to hand color—choose one with as many highlight areas as possible, since that is where color shows up best.

Hand color to add drama and depth to landscapes.

△ Use a mix of warm and cool colors to create
a three-dimensional look.

Working with Photographs of Places

Many painters take a color photograph of a scene and then use it as a reference when painting. There's a lesson to be learned here. To hand color a photograph realistically, take two photographs of the same scene—one in black and white (to hand color) and one in color (as a reference).

When hand coloring with colored pencils, experiment to determine a palette that works well for you. Use a mix of warm and cool colors to create a three-dimensional look. Try hand coloring only select areas of the print for emphasis. Achieve a surreal effect by using colors in unexpected ways: Color the grass purple or add stars or even spaceships in the sky—it's up to your imagination!

▷ Although this picture was taken on a foggy day, which might have resulted in a dark print, the ice-covered pine needles came out pale enough to hand color because they reflected the available light.

There are several things to look out for when photographing nature. Something that in person looks like the perfect subject for hand coloring may not be so ideal in a black-and-white photograph. Pine trees, for example, often appear too dark to hand color. Wait until the sun is shining directly on them before taking the photograph and the trees will appear lighter in the print. The same goes for buildings that are in shadow: They will appear darker in black and white.

As for hand coloring nature shots, since so much in nature is green, try using a palette with more than one type of green. Use yellow-green and blue-green, and create your own green by adding pink, orange, or lavender to an existing green hue.

△ The depth of the scene, the different textures in the grass, and the deer make this photograph a good candidate for hand coloring. An image with a distinct foreground, middle ground, and background offers the opportunity to enhance the illusion of depth.

Hand Coloring an Animal
in a Landscape

GETTING STARTED

Photographs of animals are wonderful to
hand color because of all the different textures in fur and feathers. For the best
results, choose an image of an animal that
is light to medium in color. This image
has been sepia-toned (see "Advanced
Techniques") to restore the warmth of the
animals' coats as well as that of the landscape. Many different colors have been
used to bring out the details in this photograph. Compare the photograph that
was not hand colored to the finished one
to observe the difference in depth. In the
hand-colored photo, the ocean appears
even farther away because of the cool
blue used on it; the colors in the middle
ground gradually increase in saturation
toward the foreground of the scene to
add dimension.

MATERIALS

○ black-and-white print on matte-surface paper

○ colored pencils: dark brown, terra-cotta, lemon
   yellow, sienna brown, light yellow-green, light
   peach, deco peach, salmon, light violet, deco blue,
   light flesh, nonphoto blue, sand, clay rose, olive
   green, dark green, pink, purple, orange

○ cotton balls

○ toothpicks

○ cotton swabs

○ turpentine-and-oil solution

○ sepia toner

 DARK BROWN

 DECO BLUE

 TERRA-COTTA

 LIGHT FLESH

LEMON YELLOW

 NONPHOTO BLUE

 SIENNA BROWN

SAND

LIGHT
YELLOW-GREEN

CLAY ROSE

 LIGHT PEACH

 OLIVE GREEN

 DECO PEACH

 DARK GREEN

 SALMON

 PINK

LIGHT VIOLET

 PURPLE

 ORANGE

▷ 1

Sepia-tone the print, then
use dark brown to color the
deer. The dark-brown pencil
is relatively soft, so solution
is not needed. After applying color to both deer, use a
cotton swab to gently rub
the pigment in.

△ 2

Use the nonphoto blue pencil to fill in the water. Smooth the color in gently with a small amount of solution. Use the sand and clay-rose pencils for the beach and sand dunes. (See "Color Mixing.") Use olive green to fill in the grass, and smooth the color in with a cotton swab. Blend the entire area with a cotton ball, but use a cotton swab at the border where the colors meet.

TIP

○ Moisten a cotton swab with water and wipe the foam areas of the ocean to pull off some of the blue and brighten the look of the water.

▷ 3

Add details and texture to the deer's coats with lemon-yellow, sienna brown, and terra-cotta pencils. Use the lemon yellow to add highlights, and use the two browns for the darker areas in the coat and around the deer's face.

◁ 4

Using a single color for an entire area tends to flatten the image. To avoid this in the grass area, add other colors either in sections, on individual blades of grass, or on random leaves. To add visual interest, use colors like pink, purple, and orange in the grass. It is important to work each color throughout the composition to help balance and unify the image as a whole.

VARIATION

Color everything but the focal point to emphasize its importance.

1. For the grass, first apply yellow-green pencil and then use light peach and deco peach for accents.
2. Color the ocean with nonphoto blue, and use blue deco on the dark parts of the waves.
3. Use a blend of the light flesh and sand pencils on the beach and the dunes.
4. Leave the deer uncolored.

△ This photo is a great example
of creating a color wash using
colored pencils in order to
cover large expanses of a
photograph.

▷ This image already has many
textures. Hand coloring, however,
gives it a lot of depth, too.

Hand Coloring Nature

GETTING STARTED

Coloring each individual leaf in the foliage area of a picture such as this one would be very time-consuming. Instead, color was added and the turpentine-and-oil solution was used to create a wash. Other colors were then used on individual leaves to create depth. A mix of dark and bright colors was used in the foreground. The blue in the sky area makes it recede into the distance. In the hilly area beneath the sky, a lighter green was used. The light green in this area produces a hazy quality, which is exactly what you see when viewing hills from a distance.

MATERIALS

- black-and-white print on matte-surface paper
- colored pencils: flesh, raw umber, terra-cotta, chartreuse, nonphoto blue, olive green, spring green, green bice, parma violet, peacock blue, dark brown, dark green, true blue
- cotton balls
- toothpicks
- cotton swabs
- turpentine-and-oil solution
- blender pencil

 FLESH   GREEN BICE

 RAW UMBER   PARMA VIOLET

 TERRA-COTTA  PEACOCK BLUE

 CHARTREUSE   DARK BROWN

 NONPHOTO BLUE DARK GREEN

OLIVE GREEN   TRUE BLUE

 SPRING GREEN

△ **1**

Color the pathway using the flesh pencil. Use a small amount of solution to smooth in the color, and use a cotton swab to pick up any excess. Use the dark-brown pencil to color the shadows created by the trees and fence in the pathway. This creates a realistic look of contrast and depth. Using a toothpick wrapped in cotton, smooth in the color so the pencil strokes are not apparent.

◁ 2

Apply a small amount of solution in the sky area, and then add nonphoto blue. Use a cotton swab to smooth in the color. (Here, the order of applying color and then solution was switched. See which way is better for you.) Don't worry if you get some blue in the leaves. Either use the blender pencil to tone down the blue in the leaves or try applying olive green to the leaves. Color the mountains using the chartreuse pencil. Using a toothpick wrapped in cotton, blend the color with solution. The color will be fairly light. There aren't many dark areas in the mountains, but the lighter wash will suggest depth.

TIP

○ Where one color meets another, a third color will be formed. To make this a smooth transition, use the blender pencil.

▷ 3

Create a color wash for the foliage instead of coloring each individual leaf. Color in one area of bushes or trees, and use a small amount of solution on a cotton swab to create an overall smoothness. Green bice was used on the bush in the foreground. The bush behind it was colored with a mixture of the dark-green and true-blue pencils. More than one layer may be necessary to create saturated, intense colors. (See "Tips for Mixing Colors.") By using the same two-color mix for the bush on the left (not shown here) a balance is created. A wash of the olive-green pencil was used in the remaining foliage. The chartreuse pencil was used to accentuate a few random leaves to create depth in the bush. The olive-green pencil was used in the remaining foliage.

◁ 4

Use the raw umber pencil to color the railing. To eliminate the pencil strokes, wrap a tiny bit of cotton dipped in a very small amount of solution on a toothpick. You can also choose not to blend it, since pencil strokes add texture. Using the terra-cotta pencil, color the trees. Use heavier layering in the tree trunks. Color the limb areas with the same pencil. There may still be a slight residual of solution on the print, so if blending is necessary, use a cotton swab. Use the spring green pencil for the foreground foliage areas. Use a cotton swab and a small amount of solution to create a wash.

VARIATION

Selective hand coloring adds emphasis to key areas of a photograph.

1. Use the parma violet pencil to color the pathway, and blend the color with a small amount of solution.
2. Using the peacock blue pencil, color the shadows of the trees on the path. Using warm and cool tones in conjunction with dark tones over lighter tones creates contrast and depth.
3. Using the peacock blue, color the railing. To add texture, let the pencil strokes remain visible.

△ This photo was chosen
because every area has
equal importance.

▷ Flowers are one of the best
subjects to hand color.
They contain many details,
which makes them great
for learning and practic-
ing different techniques.

Hand Coloring Flowers

GETTING STARTED

With any photograph, it is natural for the viewer's eye to be drawn to the lightest area of the print. Because the lightest area of this print is right on the edge, the viewer's gaze drifts off the page. To prevent this from happening and to create a tighter composition, add color to any edges that appear to be too light. Use the turpentine-and-oil solution as little as possible so the color does not become too thin. Layer the colors to make them appear more saturated and bolder.

MATERIALS

- black-and-white print on matte-surface paper
- colored pencils: salmon pink, scarlet lake, brite violet, Spanish orange, pink, grape, vermilion red, magenta, lemon yellow, deco peach, sand, metallic maroon, olive green, green bice, flesh
- cotton balls
- toothpicks
- cotton swabs
- turpentine-and-oil solution
- sepia toner

SALMON PINK   LEMON YELLOW

SCARLET LAKE   DECO PEACH

BRITE VIOLET   SAND

SPANISH   METALLIC MAROON
ORANGE

PNK   OLIVE GREEN

GRAPE   GREEN BICE

VERMILION RED   FLESH

MAGENTA

▷ 1

First, sepia-tone the photo. (See "Advanced Techniques.") Then, choose which flower to hand color first, and use salmon pink to fill it in. Notice how the flower stands out against the uncolored background. Keep in mind that since salmon pink was used in such a large area of this print, it needs to be repeated in another area to balance the color composition. Watch how the color balance shifts as different colors are added to the remaining flowers.

◁ 2

Color each flower with a base color. The palette used for this image consists mainly of pinks, peaches, and yellows. This gives it a warm, harmonious look. (See the section on choosing a palette in "The Basics.")

T I P

○ Select a palette in advance to ensure the final image appears unified in color.

▷ 3

After filling in the flower with the sand-colored pencil, use magenta in the darker areas of the flower to add depth and to tie in the colors in adjacent flowers.

◁ **4**

Using the olive-green pencil, color all the leaves. Then, use the green bice for the sprigs in front of various flowers.

VARIATION

Hand color selected areas of a toned image for a delicate look.

1. Using a sepia-toned print, color the rose with scarlet lake. Blend the color with a small amount of turpentine-and-oil solution.
2. Use olive green in the shadow areas of the rose for depth.
3. Use canary yellow in the highlight areas of the rose to add contour.
4. Color the sprigs, alternating canary yellow and green bice.
5. Color the bee with canary yellow to distinguish it from the flower.

△ The simplicity of this photograph makes it excellent for hand coloring.

▷ A large sky area allows for the application of blue, which instantly creates a three-dimensional look, since cool colors always appear to recede.

Hand Coloring Architecture

GETTING STARTED

Photographing architecture of all kinds can be great fun. You can create a personal postcard, for example, using a photo of your home, boat, or car to send to friends or family. Just have a 4 x 6 or 5 x 7 black-and-white print made on matte paper from the negative, and then add some color. On the reverse side, create the look of a store-bought postcard by adding a dividing line down the middle and lines for the address with a fine-point permanent marker. Alternatively, you can buy a premade stamp at a craft store. Keep in mind that after the photograph goes through the mail, it will have been stamped by the post office and will probably look a little worn. These nuances are part of the beauty of postcard art.

MATERIALS

- black-and-white print on matte-surface paper
- colored pencils: true blue, vermilion red, magenta, grape, blue violet, terra-cotta, brite violet, metallic purple, sand, Tuscan red
- cotton balls
- toothpicks
- cotton swabs
- turpentine-and-oil solution
- fine-point permanent marker (optional)
- transparent tape (optional)

TRUE BLUE TERRA-COTTA

VERMILION RED BRITE VIOLET

MAGENTA METALLIC PURPLE

GRAPE SAND

BLUE VIOLET TUSCAN RED

▷ 1

Begin with the sky, using the true-blue pencil.

△ 2

Enhance the mood of an image by adding different colors to the sky area. Apply vermilion red to the horizon area and magenta directly above that. Feather the two colors together so it's not apparent where one begins and the other ends.

TIPS

○ If color bleeds from one area into another, use the tip of a toothpick wrapped tightly in cotton and dampened with water to erase it or to clean up edges.

○ Try applying the turpentine-and-oil solution before applying the color. Experiment and see which order works best for you.

○ Use the solution on a cotton swab to blend in the color, and remove the pencil strokes with a cotton ball.

○ To prevent the blue sky color from bleeding into other areas, mask these areas with transparent tape and remove the tape after the color has been smoothed in.

▷ 3

Above the magenta, use the grape pencil to darken the top of the sky. This creates the illusion of depth, since it separates the top of the lighthouse from the receding sky. To enhance this effect, add blue violet along the top of the print.

◁ **4**

Use terra-cotta for the top of the lighthouse. Notice how color applied in dark areas of a print has a subtle appearance.

VARIATION

Use varied colors for a dramatic sky.

1. Mask the lighthouse with tape.
2. Start at the bottom of the sky, using the sand-colored pencil.
3. Use the pink pencil above the area colored with sand, and blend the two colors where they meet with a little solution.
4. Use the brite violet pencil above the pink.
5. Finish the sky area with the metallic purple pencil.
6. Use the sand-colored pencil in the sky around the lighthouse to make it look like it's glowing.
7. Use a cotton ball to blend the whole sky area after all the colors have been applied.
8. Remove the tape from the lighthouse. Use Tuscan red for the upper section, leaving the very top uncolored, and remove any color from the window. Color the bottom section of the lighthouse canary yellow.

ADVANCED
TECHNIQUES

With time, you'll get a feel for hand coloring and the effects it can produce. Then, consider trying another method to color black-and-white prints. Experiment with a variety of materials, such as oil paints, watercolors, or markers, to name a few. Make collages using your prints and other supplies from around the house. Some of these mediums will yield a heavier color treatment as well as texture (brushstrokes, finger marks, etc.).

Change the overall color of a print with household products such as grape juice, fabric dyes, coffee, tea, and food coloring. Anything that stains will work. Toners and nonorganic dyes are also an option. By making multiple prints of one image and trying different techniques on them, you can gain a better understanding of what effects each method produces. Keep records of what you do in case you want to re-create the result.

In this section, we'll look at toning, staining, dyeing, and painting with oils. Mix and match the different processes for different effects. By the time the artwork is finished, you may not even recognize it as having originated as a photograph!

▷ This photo was hand colored with
both oils and colored pencils.

△ Blue toner was used to change
the overall color of this image.

△ This photograph was toned and
hand colored.

Working with Other Mediums

Choose a medium based on the desired effect. To change the overall color of the print, use toner, stains, or dyes, or create a wash using pencils or oils. For a textured look, try crayons or acrylics. To obscure the image, use an opaque medium such as air brushing, spray paint, acrylics, or oil pastels. You may want to mix mediums, adding bold, graphic lines of intense color with markers or metallic pens, or coloring with oil paints and using colored pencils for fine details. Try extending the image into the white borders of the print with pen and ink. Experiment with watercolors. Liquid or tube watercolors are more vibrant and work best on fiber-based paper, but mistakes are harder to remove, and the colors fade more rapidly.

▷ Colored pencils and oils added life to this photo.

△ Oils create a dreamy effect

▽ This photograph was toned
brown and hand colored.

◁ This photograph
was simply toned.

Toners

What images tone best? Most toners are
very vibrant in color, so strong, bold
images work well. The most popular
toner is sepia toner, which gives the
image a timeless, antique look. Get a
feel for the image first, and then you'll
have a better idea of whether or not to
tone the print and which toner to use.

Toner will affect different parts of a
photo differently. White and highlight
areas in the print will take on the exact
color of the toner, but the color will
look darker in mid-tone and shadow
areas. It's a good idea to keep an extra,
untoned print handy as a reference to
gauge how heavily to tone the image.
The effects of the toner also depend on
the kind and brand of paper the photograph was printed on, whether the print
is matte or semimatte, the toner type,
how diluted the toner is, and how long
the image is toned.

If you're interested in hand coloring part
of the print after toning it, use rubber
cement to mask that part of the print
before toning. The color will be more
vibrant that way. As a rule, when combining hand coloring and toning, always
do the hand coloring last.

There are many different types and brands of toners on the market today, and photographic supply stores are the best place to find them. Some are in liquid form, some come as a powder. Some have one or two steps, some require many steps. Some toners are odorless, while others are not. Some are safe to use in the kitchen and around children, but the majority are not.

Toners can be reused if they are stored properly. Never use metal trays when working with toners, since these materials interact chemically. Use photographic trays because they are made of a heavy plastic and are meant soley for this purpose (unlike food trays).

Many toning processes include a bleach step. With these, make sure your images are 10–15% darker than they'd normally be printed. If you've never toned an image before, keep it simple: One toner per print. And remember: Always read the directions.

◁ This photograph was hand colored but not toned.

▷ Here's how it looks after it's been toned and hand colored.

Sepia Toning

GETTING STARTED

This photograph was chosen for sepia toning because the toner's brown color would lend the image warmth. It also would make the image appear timeless, giving a sense that this photograph could have been taken years ago. Toning and then hand coloring a print such as this one gives it a totally different feel, especially if it's hand colored with warm colors.

MATERIALS

○ black-and-white print on matte-surface paper, printed slightly darker than normal

○ colored pencils: nonphoto blue, spring green, hot pink, lilac, orange

○ rubber cement

○ five trays

○ two pairs of tongs

○ measuring cup

○ sepia toner

○ two dark plastic quart-size jugs for storing toner, one labeled "A," the other labeled "B"

○ rubber gloves (optional)

○ cotton swabs

○ turpentine-and-oil solution

NONPHOTO BLUE

SPRING GREEN

HOT PINK

LILAC

ORANGE

▷ 1

Follow the instructions on the package for mixing, storing, and toning the toner in a well-ventilated area away from young children. (None of this, however, needs to be done in a darkroom or under subdued light.) The toner used in this example is a two-part toner, which can be mixed in advance and stored in dark jugs. Set up five trays next to each other. The first will be a pre-wash and holding tray for prints to be toned. In the second tray, pour enough of part "A" solution, which is the bleach step. Put one set of tongs in solution "A." Use only one set of tongs for each part—don't interchange them. The third tray is for washing the print in running water in between the chemical steps. In the fourth tray, pour solution "B," the brown toner, and add a pair of tongs. The last tray will be for rinsing the print in running water when you've finished toning.

△ **2**

Bleach until the shadows start to dis-
appear. This print has been bleached
for the full amount of time. The print
will have a yellowish cast after being
bleached.

▽ **3**

The browns from the toners will fill
in the bleached areas, creating the
sepia tones.

○ When bleaching a photograph, don't worry about losing the image; the image must bleach out. Bleaching is necessary so the brown tones can exist, which is why prints you plan to sepia tone should be darker than usual.

VARIATION

Use multiple toners to make key areas stand out.

1. Rubber cement was applied to the girl before the print was toned. This prevented bleach or toner from affecting that part of the print. As a result, the masked area has the original tones, which can be colored later or left as is. To use another toner color, mask the background with rubber cement, and tone just the girl. Start by using a cotton swab to apply rubber cement to the girl.
2. Tone as per instructions and allow the print to dry.
3. Rub off the rubber cement with your finger, and finish the print by hand coloring or retoning it.

△ This print was toned using copper/red toner, which is a liquid dye. It was left in the toner for only one minute.

△ This is how the photo looked before it was toned. It is useful to keep one untoned print as a guide. Wet the toned print before comparing it to the one you're working on, because prints are slightly darker when they are wet.

○ The most noticeable effects of toning will be in the shadow areas, but check the whites to see the true color of the toner.

Toning Photographs

GETTING STARTED

Produce different effects and moods by hand coloring toned and untoned prints. Placing a toned and an untoned print side-by-side is a good way to judge the effects of these experiments. When getting started in hand coloring and toning, make more than one print and compare the results.

MATERIALS

○ black-and-white print on matte-surface paper

○ measuring cup

○ 3–4 trays

○ 1–2 pairs of tongs

○ 2–4 prints of the same image to experiment with

○ blue toner

○ red toner

○ yellow toner

▽ This print was toned for ten minutes.

△ This print was toned
with blue toner for
ten minutes.

▷ This is how the photo
looked before it
was toned.

△ This print was toned
with yellow toner
for ten minutes.

▷ This is how the photo
looked before it
was toned.

Stains

The following pages contain staining demonstrations that are wonderful projects to do with children. The products used are readily available in many households. In fact, they're typically food items, like fruit punch and coffee, that are non-toxic and can be found in the kitchen. A few stains are mixed with hot water and need to be cooled to room temperature before using (hot liquid can ruin a print).

Since stains are usually less vibrant in color than toners and dyes, select images that are more subtle. The intensity of the colors can be altered, though, by varying the concentration of the stain and the length of time the print is stained. Keep records of the dilutions used in order to create the same results with a new batch of prints. (Note the dilutions on the back of the print with a waterproof marker.) Experiment with different household foods and see which results you like the best. Try different colored fruit punches, or create your

own colors using food coloring. Try different types of teas. Regular tea, for example, creates a much deeper color stain than coffee does. Stains can be used over again. Store them in a labeled container in a cool place so they don't become moldy.

Set up a tray with water and soak the print for a minute before staining. This way, the emulsion is already saturated and will take the color as soon as it goes into the stain bath. After staining it, rinse the print in another tray of running water. (Change the water in this tray frequently.) Wash the print with room-temperature water for approximately five minutes. Take care when drying the print because stain can collect on the back or edges if dried improperly and can drip onto the image, resulting in uneven staining. Always hand color *after* dyeing or staining the prints.

△ This landscape photo
  was stained with a
  colored-pencil wash.

△ This photograph was
  stained in wine for
  ten minutes.

Staining Photographs

GETTING STARTED

Stains are usually less vibrant than toners and dyes. Select an image that contains a lot of highlights (lighter sections) and is subtle, like this photo of a boy looking out from a mass of leaves. This photo was stained with red wine at room temperature and then hand colored when it was completely dry. Some stains are made with hot water and therefore must be prepared in advance so they have time to cool to room temperature. When staining photos with food coloring or actual food or drinks (such as tea), it's okay to use kitchen trays or pans. Set up two trays: one with water, the other with stain. Use wooden or plastic tongs to keep from staining your hands.

MATERIALS

- black-and-white print on matte-surface paper
- colored pencils: crimson red, violet, scarlet lake, dark purple, chartreuse, hot pink, spring green, salmon pink, marine green, mulberry, lilac, orange
- red wine
- blue food coloring
- red punch
- coffee
- tea
- measuring cup
- glass or plastic trays large enough to accommodate prints
- cotton swabs
- turpentine-and-oil solution
- tongs

CRIMSON RED

SPRING GREEN

VIOLET

SALMON PINK

SCARLET LAKE

MARINE GREEN

DARK PURPLE

MULBERRY

CHARTREUSE

LILAC

HOT PINK

ORANGE

 1

First, prepare the surface. Immerse the print in a tray filled with water. Leave it in for one minute. Remove it from the water and put it in a tray filled with staining bath. Use your judgment as to how long to keep it in the stain. Keep a record of the amount of time you soak the print in the stain as well as of the concentration of the stain. This way, you can keep track of how you obtained your favorite results.

◁ **2**

Boil four tea bags in approximately 20 ounces (600 ml) of water, then let the tea steep until it cools to room temperature. This print was stained for ten minutes. Rinse the print for five minutes when done to remove excess tea.

▽ **3**

Brew approximately 20 ounces (600 ml) of coffee. Let it cool to room temperature. This print was stained for ten minutes. Rinse the print for five minutes when done to remove excess coffee.

TIP

○ To dry prints, use a hair dryer at a low setting or hang the prints by a corner with a clothespin. Don't lay them flat to dry because excess color and water will collect and stain parts of the print darker than the rest.

◁ **4**

Mix 10 drops of blue food coloring with 20 ounces (600 ml) of room-temperature water. Allow the picture to soak for ten minutes. Rinse the print when done to remove excess food coloring.

VARIATION

Fruit punch produces an appealingly vibrant stain.

1. Immerse the print in water in the first tray.
2. Stain the print for ten minutes in fruit punch.
3. Rinse the print and hang it to dry.

◁ Rubber cement was
applied to the stem of
the branch before this
print was dyed green for
ten minutes.

Dyes

Dyes do not chemically react with a print; instead, they dye the base color of the print. Because of this, dyes are not as permanent as toners. If a print that has been dyed is exposed to strong sunlight for any length of time, it is likely to fade. Still, dyes are sometimes desirable because they often produce more brilliant colors than stains. Photographic or liquid dyes are available at art-supply and craft stores or at photo-supply stores.

Since most dyes are vibrant, choose a photograph that is compositionally strong and graphic—one with strong lines or shapes. Also look for action shots in which someone or something is moving, which you can capture by using a fast shutter speed (or use a slow shutter speed to blur the image). Combine colors to create a hue that suits the subject matter.

Dyeing a print is fairly simple. Combine the dye with water to create a dye bath. Immerse the print in the bath. You don't need to work in a darkroom, but it is still a good idea to keep dyes out of the kitchen area and to supervise young children. Be sure to read the directions since different manufacturer's dyes are handled differently.

Remember to keep records of your experiments with dyes so you can re-create results you like. Also, the general rule of thumb for hand coloring also applies to dyeing: The print should contain a lot of highlight areas. All hand coloring should be done after dyeing or staining a print.

▽ This photograph was dyed magenta for ten minutes.

△ Hand coloring with dyes works
for this photo because Ferris
wheels are associated with
bright colors.

Dyeing Photographs

GETTING STARTED

Dyes, which are usually very vibrant, are ideal to use on photographs of brightly colored subject matter, like a Ferris wheel. To add the illusion of movement in this photo, a slow shutter speed was used when the picture was taken. The photo was hand colored using a photographic flesh-colored dye.

MATERIALS

- black-and-white print on matte-surface paper
- lemon-yellow colored pencil
- plastic tray from a photo store
- tongs (wooden or plastic)
- measuring cup
- photographic dyes: flesh, magenta, magenta mixed with cyan, green, orange
- rubber cement
- small brush

LEMON YELLOW

FLESH

MAGENTA

CYAN

GREEN

ORANGE

△ 1

Prepare the surface by soaking the photograph in a tray of fresh water for at least one minute.

○ Make sure to use fresh water
and clean tongs when you go
from one colored dye to the
next. Staining or contamina-
tion can occur if you're not
careful.

△ **2**

Prepare a tray with 20 ounces
(600 ml) of room-temperature
water. Add 10 drops of dye (in
this case, orange) to the water
and mix with the tongs. Make
sure the color is evenly dispersed.
After dyeing, wash the print in a
tray of fresh tap water at room
temperature for five minutes.
Hang the print to dry or use a
blow dryer at a low setting. This
print was dyed for eight minutes.

▷ **3**

Try combining different colors to
create a new one. This color was
created by mixing 5 ounces (150 ml)
of magenta with 5 ounces of cyan in
20 ounces (600 ml) of water. The
print was dyed for ten minutes.

△ **4**

Mix 10 drops of green dye into 20 ounces (600 ml) of water. This print was dyed for eight minutes.

VARIATION

Contrasting colors bring out a picture's highlights.

1. Rubber cement was used as a mask to cover the lights on the Ferris wheel so they could be hand colored separately, adding color contrast to this image.
2. Pre-wash the print. Then, soak it in dye for eight minutes and allow it to dry.
3. Rub off the rubber cement with your finger, and hand color the lights using the lemon-yellow pencil.

▷ Some black-and-white postcards are perfect for hand coloring with oils.

Oils

Hand coloring with oils can produce a much different effect than using colored pencils. For starters, oil colors are slightly more intense and vibrant. Also, oils are noted for their permanence.

There are many different types of oil paints. Photographic oils are designed specifically for hand coloring prints. Oils can be used on a semimatte or matte paper, but if you plan to do detail work with colored pencils afterward, you'll need to work on matte paper. If you use artist's oil paints, try thinning the oils with transparentizing gel before using them. This will make them more transparent without affecting the intensity of the colors. Another option is to use extender, which can be added to oil paint to reduce color intensity.

Like pencils, oils are, for the most part, easy to remove (although some of the more vibrant colors do not come off so easily). Gently rub mistakes away with a cotton swab or cotton ball, or use the turpentine-and-oil solution or mineral spirits. If the print has white borders, protect them with transparent tape. This is also a fingerprint-free means of holding the photo down while you work on it.

▷ This postcard was colored blue with a wash of oil paint.

△ A good candidate for hand coloring, this photograph has strong elements in the foreground (the leaves) and a lot of depth.

First, prepare the print surface; otherwise, the colors may appear too strong. Using a cotton ball, apply a small amount of either mineral spirits or turpentine-and-oil solution directly to the print surface. (Resin-coated paper requires less solution than fiber-based.)

Using a palette, whether it is store-bought or just a plastic plate, is recommended. Place small amounts of oil paint directly on it and mix the colors with a toothpick. It's difficult to exactly re-create a mixed color, so be sure to mix more than you think you'll need.

Save any left-over color by putting the palette in a sealable plastic bag. Oils can take hours or days to dry anyway, depending on how thickly they have been applied, but the plastic bag is an extra measure to prevent them from drying. This way, you can come back to your print later to add more color.

Use cotton swabs to dab color directly
from the palette onto the print surface.
For large areas, use a cotton ball to
work the color in. For the smallest
areas, use a cotton swab or wrap a
toothpick with cotton and use it as a
paintbrush. For very fine details, try
using the end of a plain toothpick (but
don't press down hard with the toothpick—this can scratch the emulsion of
the print).

Layering colors will increase their intensity, but allow time for each layer to dry
before adding another or the paint
might crack.

▽ Oils were used to color the
large areas, such as the
grass, and colored pencils
were used to punch up the
small details, like the leaves.

◁ The beauty of hand coloring
this image is its simplicity,
yet a lot of detail work can
be added to the tulips.

Adding Subtle Details with Oils

GETTING STARTED

These tulips were photographed on top of a piece of black velvet to enhance the contrast. When working with large dark areas, like the background in this picture, wear nylon or cotton gloves, or place a piece of soft gauze between your hand and the surface of the print. This will prevent the oils from your hands from leaving marks in the dark sections. Start by adding color to the large areas of the flowers and end by doing the fine detail work. This is a great picture in which to mix mediums. Color the flowers and stems with oils, and add details in the flowers with either oils or pencils.

MATERIALS

- black-and-white print on matte-surface paper
- oils: yellow, yellow-green, warm red, cadmium orange, dioxazine purple, chartreuse, imperial violet
- cotton balls
- toothpicks
- cotton swabs
- turpentine-and-oil solution
- palette
- gloves

YELLOW   DIOXAZINE PURPLE

YELLOW-GREEN   CHARTREUSE

WARM RED   IMPERIAL VIOLET

CADMIUM ORANGE

▷ 1

Start with a semimatte or matte print. (Use a flat matte print if you plan to also use pencils.) Select your colors and place a small amount of each on a palette.

◁ 2

Treat the surface of both tulips with solution. Apply imperial violet oil from the palette to the top tulip with a cotton swab. Use a circular motion to work the oil in so that it is smooth.

▷ 3

Apply a small amount of warm red to a second tulip to complement the coolness of the imperial violet tulip, using the same circular motion with a cotton swab. Continue to use clean swabs until all the color is smoothed in.

▷ 4

Use a toothpick wrapped tightly with cotton to apply a very small amount of yellow-green from the palette to the stems of the tulips. (It is not necessary to prepare the print surface of the stems for this step.) Have a few more toothpicks with cotton already made. Work back and forth until all the color is blended. If you accidentally get some of the color in the background area, erase it with a cotton swab moistened with a very small amount of water.

◁ 5

Flowers contain a lot of green. Extend the green from the stem up into the darker (shadow) areas of the flowers. Apply color with a toothpick wrapped tightly with cotton, following the shading in the flower. A very small amount of warm red (the same color as the bottom tulip) was used in the highlights of the top tulip, and yellow was used in the bottom tulip in the lighter areas. Using another color gives the flowers depth.

TIPS

○ Keep in mind that the same color oil paint can differ in appearance from manufacturer to manufacturer.

○ Layer colors for a more saturated look. Allow each layer to dry before adding another.

VARIATION

Build up colors for a textured look.

A heavier application of color was used for this variation. The color appears to sit on the surface, giving the image a bolder quality. The buildup of color also adds texture. The print surface was not prepared beforehand, so the colors stayed opaque.

1. Color the background using red oil applied with a cotton ball (use a cotton swab near the flower areas). Here, cadmium orange was used in the lighter areas of the background.
2. Using a cotton swab, apply dioxazine purple to the bottom tulip. Dab the color on without smoothing it in.
3. Apply cadmium orange to the top tulip with a cotton swab, and smooth it in a bit. Dab all over with a cotton ball, getting some of the color to go outside the lines of the flower. The feathering of orange in the background of this picture was created by the fibers from the cotton ball.
4. Use green to color in the stem, using the same technique as on the other stems.

△ Coloring the wispy clouds
adds mood and depth
to this photo.

◁ Oils work in expansive areas
(in this case, the sky and
sand dunes) as well as in
small areas (the kite and
its tail).

Hand Coloring Expansive
Areas with Oils

GETTING STARTED

Prepare the print surface with either
mineral spirits or the turpentine-and-oil
solution, which is also used with colored
pencils. (It's very important to use very
small amounts of these solutions and to
coat the print evenly.) Squirt a small
amount of the oil colors that will be used
to hand color the image onto a palette.
You will be using the colors directly from
the palette.

MATERIALS

- ○ black-and-white print on matte-surface paper

- ○ oils: sepia, ultramarine blue, cadmium orange,
  magenta, lemon yellow, crimson red, cadmium
  green, pink

- ○ cotton balls

- ○ toothpicks

- ○ cotton swabs

- ○ turpentine-and-oil solution

- ○ blender pencil

- ○ artist's palette

- ○ transparent tape

SEPIA

LEMON YELLOW

ULTRAMARINE
BLUE

CRIMSON RED

CADMIUM
ORANGE

CADMIUM GREEN

MAGENTA

PINK

▷ 1

Use a cotton swab to dab the sepia oil
onto the dunes. With a fresh cotton swab,
smooth the color in. Do not allow color to
collect in areas. Keep using fresh cotton
swabs until you have a smooth layer of
color. If necessary, add more layers of
color later for greater saturation.

◁ **2**

With a cotton swab, color the entire sky area and kite with ultramarine blue. Use circular motions to smooth it in. Don't worry about color bleeding into the clouds, fence, or kite.

TIP

○ Use the blender pencil to erase unwanted colors.

△ **3**

Use a cotton swab to color the clouds in the upper-left portion of the photograph with cadmium orange, and smooth it in. For balance, use the same color for the clouds in the lower right. Use magenta for the cloud in the middle of the picture, applying the color with a cotton swab. For the wisps of clouds near the dunes, use lemon yellow applied with a toothpick wrapped in a small amount of cotton.

▷ **4**

After the paint has dried, go back into the clouds with the same colors and add another layer of color for a deeper, richer look. Gently run a toothpick dipped in water along the fencing to erase the blue color. Be careful not to scratch the print's surface. With a clean toothpick, do the same in the tail of the kite. Dip a clean toothpick wrapped in cotton in a small amount of water. With your fingers, squeeze out any excess water. Erase the blue in the kite. Notice that, without color, the kite and fencing stand out more.

VARIATION

Oil paints are ideal for textured detail work.

1. Prepare the print's surface by applying the turpentine-and-oil solution with a toothpick wrapped in a small amount of cotton. Use the solution very sparingly.
2. Prepare your palette.
3. Apply a small amount of lemon yellow to the kite with a toothpick wrapped in cotton. Apply crimson red with a fresh toothpick (not wrapped in cotton). Apply crimson red to one section of the kite's tail. Then, using the same procedure, add cadmium green and pink to the other sections of the tail.

CREATING
SPECIAL
EFFECTS

Now it's time to experiment and really play. You have a basic understanding of hand coloring and have learned with materials that are very forgiving, will erase easily, and are easy to apply to a print. This is your foundation. Now try mixing various mediums to create textures or even to totally obscure the image. Continue to avoid glossy paper. Remember that many mediums can be applied to a semimatte surface, but in order to use pencils, matte paper is still required. Most materials are either water-based (watercolor paints, retouching dyes, tempera, gouache,

acrylics, pen and ink) or oil-based (oil paints, photo oils, oil sticks, oil pastels, oil-based markers). Other options include colored pencils, crayons, and markers. Some are transparent, and some are opaque. Different materials can be mixed, but be careful: The water-based materials can erase or dissolve pencils and oils, and the solvent used with pencils and oils can erase or dissolve watercolors. The gallery sections that follow offer many examples of different hand-coloring techniques—everything from using markers to making collages. No two look the same!

▽ Mix mediums to balance a textured background painted with acrylics and delicate subject matter colored with markers.

◁ *Katie*
by Amy Jean Rowan
Here, Rowan used permanent markers, oil sticks, oil pastels, and charcoal.

Markers

Markers are great fun to work with, and there are lots of varieties to choose from. There are water-based, solvent-based, or oil-based markers, and there are many colors and point ranges (from fine tip to broad tip). Markers are fairly permanent, so be sure that what you put down on paper is what you want. To thin the markers and make them easier to apply, try using a clear blender marker, which most art-supply stores carry. The blender also extends the ink's drying time, makes it somewhat transparent, and makes it possible to mix colors. Without the blender, the marker acts as an opaque medium and dries immediately. Rarely are markers used exclusively to hand color a photograph. Instead, they're usually used in just a section or two.

▽ *Bus Stop*
by Amy Jean Rowan
Rowan used oil pastels and a
paint pen to color this image.

October 23, 1997
by Amy Jean Rowan
Rowan made a photocopy
of a Polaroid transfer and
colored it with markers.

△ *Ferris Wheel*
by Amy Jean Rowan
Rowan used a combination of
gesso, oil pastels, pastels, Conté
crayons, and a paint pen on this
color photograph.

From *Pastoral Interludes* series
by Kate and Geir Jordahl
The photographs in this series were hand
colored with colored pencils and acrylics.

Acrylics

Although acrylics come in a variety of
bold and vibrant colors, they can have a
flat appearance on a print. To avoid dull
color, thickly apply substantial amounts
of paint to create texture, or add another
medium on top of the acrylics. Before
they dry, acrylics are easy to remove with
water, but once dry (and they dry very
quickly), they're very durable. Normally,
acrylics are very opaque, but since they're
water-based, they can be combined with
water for a more transparent look.

◁ *Untitled*
by Laurie Klein
This cyanotype was made
from a glass positive found
at a flea market. A contact
print of it was made and
hand colored with water-
color pencil.

Watercolors

Watercolors are popular with hand colorists because they're translucent and can be used to create delicate washes of color. Tube watercolors produce deeper color than watercolor cakes, are easier to apply, and can be erased with small amounts of water. Liquid watercolors are very hard to remove and fade quickly, but they're incredibly vibrant in color. Watercolors in general work best on fiber-based paper. Apply watercolors with paintbrushes or cotton swabs, and prepare the colors on a palette. Also available are water-based crayons and pencils. These can be applied directly to a print and smoothed in with a cotton swab (or not smoothed in if texture is desired). Watercolors can often appear subtle, but layers can be added for greater intensity. Be sure to let each layer dry before adding another.

△ *Untitled*
by Jane Page-Conway
The artist first tones her photographs and
then hand colors them with watercolors.

△ *Untitled*
by Jane Page-Conway
The artist first tones her photographs and
then hand colors them with watercolors.

△ *Untitled*
by Jane Page-Conway

◁ *Home*
by Mary McCarthy
McCarthy cut up a hand-
colored black-and-white
photograph and collaged
the pieces into a "quilt."

Mixed Media

Many hand colorists use alternative film
processes. Instead of making a silver
photographic print, many make their
own emulsions or buy premade emulsion and paint or coat a piece of paper
with it. This process gives the print a
handmade, tactile look, but the negative
needs to be the size of the image you
want to produce. Palladium and plat-
inum printing are also quite popular.
These prints have a silvery quality. Van
Dyke prints are brownish in color, and
cyanotypes are like blue prints. Very
popular these days are Polaroid or
image transfers that are transferred onto
cold- or hot-pressed watercolor paper
and then hand colored. Many artists create collages and integrate hand coloring
into the piece. Collages can be created
using a variety of materials, such as
photocopies of old family snapshots,
pictures cut out from magazines, old
postcards, images that have been sewn
together, or handmade paper or fabric.

△ *Untitled*
by Jane Page-Conway
This image was toned with a mix
of acrylics, oils, and pastels.

△ *Alyssa*
by Bobi Eldridge
Eldridge made a Polaroid
transfer and then hand
colored it with colored
pencils and tempera.

△ *West Point Lighthouse*
by Bobi Eldridge
Eldridge made a Polaroid
transfer and then hand
colored it with colored
pencils and tempera.

Directory of Artists

Bobi Eldridge
P. O. Box 1702
Orleans, MA 02653

Mary McCarthy
249 A Street, No. 25
Boston, MA 02210

Kate and Geir Jordahl
144 Medford Avenue
Hayward, CA 94541

Jane Page-Conway
13 Wildes Road
Bowdoinham, ME 04008

Laurie Klein
Laurie Klein Gallery
290 Federal Road
Brookfield, CT 06804

Amy Jean Rowan
52 Blueberry Lane
Bridgewater, CT 06752

Index

Acknowledgments

I would like to thank all of my family, who have always told me there isn't anything I can't do. Many of the photographs in this book are pictures of them. I especially want to thank my sons, Kyle and Bryce, for their patience and support. Thank you also to my clients, who not only gave permission but encouraged me to use their photographs for this book. I received much assistance from the women who work with me at the Laurie Klein Gallery: Ellen and Amy helped me put my thoughts on paper (Ellen aslo organized much of the material and was there when I needed an extra hand), and Jennifer kept the Laurie Klein Gallery running smoothly while I was occupied with this project; and Fred, a friend and my accountant, looked out for me and the bottom line. Thank you Mary McCarthy for helping me find Rockport and to all at Rockport, especially Kristina, Shawna, and Martha. Lastly, I want to thank my companion, Gordon, who helps me enjoy and make sense of my journey and encourages me to be all that I am, including the author of this labor of love. Much love to you all.

—LJK

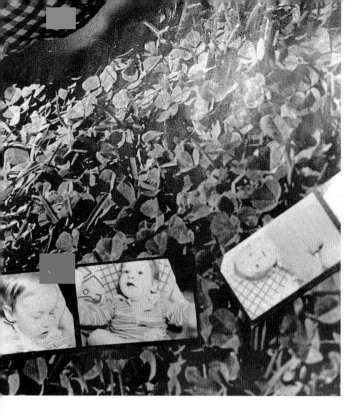

About the Author

Laurie Klein lives in Brookfield,
Connecticut, where she operates the
Laurie Klein Gallery. Laurie specializes in
portrait and wedding photography. She
shoots predominantly in black and white
and then hand colors the photographs.
Laurie has traveled throughout the country
for her work. She is a protégée of Ansel
Adams and has taught photography to
amateur and professional photographers
for eighteen years. Her method for hand
coloring her creative compositions was
recently featured on Lifetime's *Our Home*
show. Laurie's lovely images have also
been featured in numerous magazines
and books and in a line of greeting cards,
and her fine-art work has been exhibited
internationally. Sanford Corporation, which
makes the colored pencils she uses, has
sponsored Laurie for a number of years.